Date	Name	Comments

Date	Name	Comments

Date	Name	Comments

Date	Name	Comments

Date	Name	Comments

Date	Name	Comments

Date	Name	Comments

Date	Name	Comments

Date	Name	Comments

Date	Name	Comments

Date	Name	Comments

Date	Name	Comments

Date	Name	Comments

Date	Name	Comments

Date	Name	Comments

Date	Name	Comments

Date	Name	Comments

Date	Name	Comments

Date	Name	Comments

Date	Name	Comments

Date	Name	Comments

Date	Name	Comments

Date	Name	Comments

Date	Name	Comments

Date	Name	Comments

Date	Name	Comments

Date	Name	Comments

Date	Name	Comments

Date	Name	Comments

Date	Name	Comments

Date	Name	Comments

Date	Name	Comments

Date	Name	Comments

Date	Name	Comments

Date	Name	Comments

Date	Name	Comments

Date	Name	Comments

Date	Name	Comments

Date	Name	Comments

Date	Name	Comments

Date	Name	Comments

Date	Name	Comments

Date	Name	Comments

Date	Name	Comments

Date	Name	Comments

Date	Name	Comments

Date	Name	Comments

Date	Name	Comments

Date	Name	Comments

Date	Name	Comments

Date	Name	Comments

Date	Name	Comments

Date	Name	Comments

Date	Name	Comments

Date	Name	Comments

Date	Name	Comments

Date	Name	Comments

Date	Name	Comments

Date	Name	Comments

Date	Name	Comments

Date	Name	Comments

Date	Name	Comments

Date	Name	Comments

Date	Name	Comments

Date	Name	Comments

Date	Name	Comments

Date	Name	Comments

Date	Name	Comments

Date	Name	Comments

Date	Name	Comments

Date	Name	Comments

Date	Name	Comments

Date	Name	Comments

Date	Name	Comments

Date	Name	Comments

Date	Name	Comments

Date	Name	Comments

Date	Name	Comments

Date	Name	Comments

Date	Name	Comments

Date	Name	Comments

Date	Name	Comments

Date	Name	Comments

Date	Name	Comments

Date	Name	Comments

Date	Name	Comments

Date	Name	Comments

Date	Name	Comments

Date	Name	Comments

Date	Name	Comments

Date	Name	Comments

Date	Name	Comments

Date	Name	Comments

Date	Name	Comments

Date	Name	Comments

Date	Name	Comments

Date	Name	Comments

Date	Name	Comments

Date	Name	Comments

Date	Name	Comments

Date	Name	Comments

Date	Name	Comments

Date	Name	Comments

Date	Name	Comments

Date	Name	Comments

Date	Name	Comments

Date	Name	Comments

Date	Name	Comments

Date	Name	Comments

Date	Name	Comments

Date	Name	Comments

Date	Name	Comments

Date	Name	Comments

Date	Name	Comments

Date	Name	Comments

Date	Name	Comments

Date	Name	Comments

Date	Name	Comments

Date	Name	Comments

Date	Name	Comments

Date	Name	Comments

Date	Name	Comments

Date	Name	Comments

Date	Name	Comments

Date	Name	Comments

Date	Name	Comments

Date	Name	Comments

Date	Name	Comments

Date	Name	Comments

Date	Name	Comments

Date	Name	Comments

Date	Name	Comments

Date	Name	Comments

Date	Name	Comments

Date	Name	Comments

Date	Name	Comments

Date	Name	Comments

Date	Name	Comments

Date	Name	Comments

Date	Name	Comments

Date	Name	Comments

Date	Name	Comments

Date	Name	Comments

Date	Name	Comments

Date	Name	Comments

Date	Name	Comments

Date	Name	Comments

Date	Name	Comments

Date	Name	Comments

Date	Name	Comments

Date	Name	Comments

Date	Name	Comments

Date	Name	Comments

Date	Name	Comments

Date	Name	Comments

Date	Name	Comments

Date	Name	Comments

Date	Name	Comments

Date	Name	Comments

Date	Name	Comments

Date	Name	Comments

Date	Name	Comments

Date	Name	Comments

Date	Name	Comments

Date	Name	Comments

Date	Name	Comments

Date	Name	Comments

Date	Name	Comments

Date	Name	Comments

Date	Name	Comments

Date	Name	Comments

Date	Name	Comments

Date	Name	Comments

Date	Name	Comments

Date	Name	Comments

Date	Name	Comments